Essential
Easter
Prayers

PARACLETE PRESS

PARACLETE PRESS
BREWSTER, MASSACHUSETTS

2021 First Printing

Essential Easter Prayers

Copyright © 2021 by Paraclete Press, Inc.

ISBN 978-1-64060-660-9

The excerpts from published books shown in the text are published by Paraclete Press, Brewster, MA 02653.

The Paraclete Press name and logo (dove on cross) are trademarks of Paraclete Press.

    Library of Congress Cataloging-in-Publication Data
Names: Paraclete Press, editor.
Title: Essential Easter prayers.
Description: Brewster, Massachusetts : Paraclete Press, 2021. | Summary: "A
  companion book for anyone celebrating the season of Easter, prayers and
  practices from a variety of denominations and traditions"-- Provided by
  publisher.
Identifiers: LCCN 2020036589 (print) | LCCN 2020036590 (ebook) | ISBN
  9781640606609 | ISBN 9781640606616 (epub) | ISBN 9781640606623 (pdf)
Subjects: LCSH: Eastertide--Prayers and devotions.
Classification: LCC BV55 .E77 2021 (print) | LCC BV55 (ebook) | DDC
  242.8--dc23
LC record available at https://lccn.loc.gov/2020036589
LC ebook record available at https://lccn.loc.gov/2020036590

10 9 8 7 6 5 4 3 2 1

Published by Paraclete Press
Brewster, Massachusetts
www.paracletepress.com

Printed in the United States of America

"We are an Easter people
and Alleluia is our song."

—*St. Pope John Paul II*

CONTENTS

Dedication to the Resurrected Life

9

INTRODUCTION

11

It's Friday, But Sunday's Coming

13

Easter Vigil Prayers

27

Pascha-themed Prayers

43

He Is Risen

55

Prayers for Eastertide

71

CONTRIBUTOR BIOGRAPHIES

91

Dedication to the Resurrected Life

Christ has no body now, but yours.
No hands, no feet on earth, but yours.
Yours are the eyes through which
Christ looks compassion into the world.
Yours are the feet
with which Christ walks to do good.
Yours are the hands
with which Christ blesses the world.

—*St. Teresa of Avila*

INTRODUCTION

Easter is a time of new birth, joy, and song. Following on the heels of Lent, when the church is made dark, and when our lives are filled with introspection, refocus, and attention to fasting, penance, and prayer, Easter is by sudden and delightful contrast a time for celebration.

Alleluia!

The title of the first section of this book is inspired by a famous sermon preached by S. M. Lockridge, an African American pastor of the twentieth century, which was also made popular by Christian author and preacher Tony Campolo. Friday is the worst, saddest day in history for a disciple of Jesus; on that day, 2,000 some years ago, no one knew that Sunday was coming. But, then, what happened on Sunday?—the victory of the Resurrection.

This is followed by Easter Vigil, or Holy Saturday, prayers. We often feel that the day between Good Friday and Easter is the strangest, most mysterious day on the Christian liturgical calendar. The horrific execution and suffering of our Lord on Friday is followed on Saturday by an even deeper expression of his love for us, his descent into hell. We won't even attempt to unpack what this means in all of its nuance—theologians have long debated it—but the prayers in this section of the book will help you meet and understand Christ on this unusual day. Dedicate your Holy Saturday to prayer, if you can.

"Pascha-themed Prayers" offers a reminder to us of how poorly the English word *Easter* communicates what the season of Easter is all about. In Greek and Latin, and many other languages around the world, the word for the season and feast of Easter is a word associated with Passover, indelibly linking the Christian and Jewish holidays. The prayers you will find in this section are most common in Eastern Orthodox and Eastern Catholic churches where the Pascha theme is present. As you will see, in the recognition and celebration of Christ's triumph over death, these prayers continue the themes of Holy Saturday.

Then, "He Is Risen" and "Prayers for Eastertide" will focus you on what is supposed to happen in and through each of us, as a result of our identification with the Christ who suffered death and was buried, and then rose again, in accordance with the Scriptures.

Throughout this season, as you use this little book, may your life be full of resurrection renewal and glory.

—*The Editors at Paraclete Press*

It's Friday,
But Sunday's Coming

Pain and Joy

Dear God,
With Julian of Norwich I lament
the suffering of my Lord.
"Of all pains that lead to salvation this is
the most pain, to see thy Love suffer.
How might any pain be more to me than to see
Him that is all my life, all my bliss,
and all my joy,
suffer?"
O Lord, dear God, thank You
that Sunday
is coming soon.

—A new prayer, using the words of Julian of Norwich
adapted from The Complete Julian of Norwich

Lord, Into Your Hands I Commit My Spirit

In you, Lord, I have taken refuge;
let me never be put to shame;
deliver me in your righteousness.
Turn your ear to me,
come quickly to my rescue;
be my rock of refuge,
strong fortress to save me.
Since you are my rock and my fortress,
for the sake of your name lead and guide me.
Keep me free from the trap that is set for me,
for you are my refuge.
Into your hands I commit my spirit;
deliver me, Lord, my faithful God.

—Psalm 31:1–5 (NIV)

Franciscan Prayer for Walking the Via Dolorosa *"Way of Suffering"*

We adore you, O Christ,
and we bless you.

Because by your holy cross,
you have redeemed the world.

*The Via Dolorosa is a processional route in the
Old City of Jerusalem—the path Jesus walked
to the Crucifixion. There are fourteen stations along
the way; this prayer is repeated fourteen times.*

St. Paul's Prayer

Dear God,
"It is no longer I who live,
but it is Christ who lives in me.
And the life I now live in the flesh I live
by faith in the Son of God,
who loved me and
gave himself
for me."

—*Galatians 2:20*

To the One Who Died on the Cross

O my Lord and Savior, in Thy arms I am safe; keep me and I have nothing to fear; give me up and I have nothing to hope for. I know not what will come upon me before I die. I know nothing about the future, but I rely upon Thee. I pray Thee to give me what is good for me; I pray Thee to take from me whatever may imperil my salvation; I pray Thee not to make me rich, I pray Thee not to make me very poor; but I leave it all to Thee, because Thou knowest and I do not. If Thou bringest pain or sorrow on me, give me grace to bear it well—keep me from fretfulness and selfishness. If Thou givest me health and strength and success in this world, keep me ever on my guard lest these great gifts carry me away from Thee. O Thou who didst die on the Cross for me, even for me, sinner as I am, give me to know Thee, to believe on Thee, to love Thee, to serve Thee; ever to aim at setting forth Thy glory; to live to and for Thee; to set a good example to all around me; give me to die just at that time and in that way which is most for Thy glory, and best for my salvation.

—St. John Henry Newman

Remind Me Today and Every Day

O Jesus, my Lord!
Remind me today, and every day, how
"Christ is Christ only as the suffering and rejected one,
so the disciple is a disciple only as
one who suffers and is rejected,
as one crucified with Jesus."

—*A new prayer, incorporating words of Dietrich Bonhoeffer*

When She Despairs
(after Wendell Berry)

When she despairs, knowing how
each thing she loves will one day end,
she goes down to the river's edge,
lets otters remind her of play
salmon of perseverance
cormorant of stillness.

She watches how sun and water
create gold and silver in a flash
and forgets her worries,
suddenly sees she is swan's wings
on a winter wind, bud on the blackthorn
branch, ready to break into blossom.

—*Christine Valters-Paintner,*
From The Wisdom of Wild Grace: Poems

Prayer of Abandonment

Father, I abandon myself into your hands,
do with me what you will.
Whatever you may do, I thank you.
I am ready for all, I accept all.
Let only your Will be done in me,
and in all your creatures,
I wish no more than this, O Lord.
Into your hands I commend my soul.
I offer it to you, with all the love of my heart,
For I love you, and so need to give myself,
to surrender myself into your hands
without reserve, and with boundless confidence,
for you are my Father.

—*Bl. Charles de Foucauld*

Devotion to the Black Nazarene

When you feel you are alone, and you have no one to
hold on to . . . have faith.
Hold on to Jesus. Jesus is carrying you.
He will not let you astray, even if His shoulders are wounded.
He is carrying you. He is holding you.
And while He is holding you, He thanks God.
You are not heavy. You are not a burden.

—Cardinal Luis Antonio Tagle
(January 9, 2015)

The Black Nazarene is a life-sized image of Christ,
kneeling, carrying the cross. Devotion to Christ
through this image is common in the Philippines.

Hold On

Bambelela.	Hold on.
Bambelela.	Hold on.
Bambelela.	Hold on.
Bambelela.	Hold on.
Ku Jesu Bambelela.	Hold on to Jesus.
Ku Jesu Bambelela.	Hold on to Jesus.
Ku Jesu Bambelela.	Hold on to Jesus.
Ku Jesu Bambelela.	Hold on to Jesus.

—A popular Zulu Gospel song in South Africa.
With slight variants, also common in other
Christian parts of Africa, especially Nigeria.

A Prayer for Faith and Courage

I'm going to hold steady on You, an'
You've got to see me through.

—*Harriet Tubman*

Easter Vigil Prayers

These words we pray as we wait upon our Lord
who was gruesomely crucified on a cross,
and buried in a tomb, before he rises again.

Prayers for Light in Times of Darkness

1

O God our Father, hear me, while I am trembling in this darkness, and stretch forth Your hand to me. Hold out Your light before me. Save me from my wanderings, and, with You as my guide, may I be restored to myself and to You, through Jesus Christ. Amen.

2

You are the Lord—the Light, the Way, the Truth, the Life, in whom there is no darkness, wandering, error, or death. You are the Light without which there is darkness, the Way without which there is wandering, the Truth without which there is error, the Life without which there is death. Lord, let me see the light; show me the way; reveal to me truth; and allow me to escape death. Illuminate my blind soul that sits in darkness and the shadow of death and direct my feet in the way of peace.

3

May the light of my heart, not my own darkness, speak to me now. I fell off, and became darkened, but even so, I loved You. I went astray, but I remembered You. I heard Your voice behind me, calling me to return, and scarcely heard it, through the tumultuousness of the enemies of peace. Now, I return in distress and panting after Your fountain, to drink, and to live. Leave me not to myself, but revive me in You.

—*St. Augustine of Hippo*

Holy Saturday in the Bible

In the Scriptures we don't find Holy Saturday as we've come to know it in the church, but there it is in the Apostle's Creed:

> I believe in God, the Father Almighty,
> Creator of Heaven and earth;
> and in Jesus Christ, His only Son Our Lord,
> Who was conceived by the Holy Spirit,
> born of the Virgin Mary,
> suffered under Pontius Pilate,
> was crucified, died, and was buried.
> *He descended into Hell;*
> the third day He rose again from the dead ...

Holy Saturday is the day after Good Friday when Jesus lay in the tomb, but in some very real way, as his body lay wrecked, his spirit too was troubled to death to the point of descending into hell itself. There, according to tradition, and according to paintings and depictions of all kinds throughout the centuries, we see Christ "trampling the gates" of hell, demonstrating that he has broken the bonds of death once and for all time for those who believe.

When we celebrate an Easter Vigil, whether in church or on our own in prayer, we begin in the quiet and anticipation of "being with" our Lord in the tomb, and then gloriously witnessing the revelation of his resurrection as the night of Saturday turns to the first stroke of Easter Sunday.

A Conversation Prayer

What am I supposed to do
today, Lord?
Christ, where have You gone?
What am I to do, now?
I have heard people criticize your disciples, the one who
denied You, the one who insisted on evidences in order to believe,
But I can't criticize. They are me.
Please, I pray, keep preparing me for
Your Resurrection.

Resurrection Fruit

I caught the fruit before they pinned me in harlequin time,
and ate it whole: a small, ripe sun, a joy inside my ribs
when the pitch-black storm riddled my heart
and made a riddle of souls I sheltered there.

But even as I rose and sank on the bleeding tree,
as the wind shrieked denials to my fraying will
and the howling hills drew close to savage their spoil,
I felt a current escorting me up from the fret of flesh,

the faces of scorn and desire, from the wrecked
earth full of bones I know will live, O Glory!
How strong the ladder of Your arms to raise me
shivering, newborn, into jubilation bursting forever.

—*Suzanne Underwood Rhodes*
from Flying Yellow: New and Selected Poems

Traditional Byzantine Matins Prayer on Holy Saturday

Today, the One who holds all creation in his hand
is himself held in the tomb.
A rock covers the One who covered the heavens with beauty.
Life has fallen asleep.
Hades is seized with fear,
and Adam is freed from his bonds.
Glory to Your work of salvation;
through it you have accomplished the eternal Sabbath rest,
and You grant us the gift of your holy Resurrection.

For Lighting a Candle

O truly blessed night,

worthy alone to know the time and hour

when Christ rose from the underworld!

This is the night of which it is written:

The night shall be as bright as day,

dazzling is the night for me, and full of gladness.

The sanctifying power of this night

dispels wickedness, washes faults away,

restores innocence to the fallen, and joy to mourners,

drives out hatred, fosters concord, and brings down the mighty.

On this, your night of grace, O holy Father,

accept this candle, a solemn offering,

the work of bees and of your servants' hands,

an evening sacrifice of praise,

this gift from your most holy Church.

O Truly Blessed Night

O truly blessed night,
when things of heaven are wed to those of earth,
and divine to the human.
Therefore, O Lord, we pray you that this candle,
hallowed to the honor of your name,
may persevere undimmed,
to overcome the darkness of this night.
Receive it as a pleasing fragrance,
and let it mingle with the lights of heaven.
May this flame be found still burning
by the Morning Star: the one Morning Star who never sets,
Christ your Son, who, coming back from death's domain,
has shed his peaceful light on humanity,
and lives and reigns for ever and ever.

—From the Roman Missal

For a Night Vigil with Fire

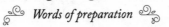 *Words of preparation*

On this most sacred night,
in which our Lord Jesus Christ
passed over from death to life,
the Church calls upon her sons and daughters,
scattered throughout the world,
to come together to watch and pray.
If we keep the memorial
of the Lord's paschal solemnity in this way,
listening to his word and celebrating his mysteries,
then we shall have the sure hope
of sharing his triumph over death
and living with him in God.

LET US PRAY.

O God, who through your Son
bestowed upon the faithful the fire of your glory,
sanctify this new fire, we pray, and grant that,
by these paschal celebrations,
we may be so inflamed with heavenly desires,
that with minds made pure
we may attain festivities of unending splendor,
through Christ our Lord. Amen.

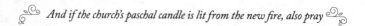 *And if the church's paschal candle is lit from the new fire, also pray*

May the light of Christ
rising in glory
dispel the darkness of our
hearts and minds.

—*From ibreviary.com*

A prayer request of Mother Teresa to an American priest visiting Calcutta

Father, please
pray for me –
where is Jesus?

St. Teresa of Calcutta lived for decades in a kind of spiritual darkness, keeping faith without feeling the presence of God.

Easter

In the tomb
his cheek ashens,
the silence stiffens.
When will his cells enliven,
his blood begin its orbit,
his skin pinken?
When will he flex and rise
into the dawn of new time?

He quickens, infused with tempo,
his heartbeat
breaking through the grave's secrets
crushing the silence,
trampling death.

And he rises.
he rises indeed,
light blazing.

—Jill Peláez Baumgaertner
from From Shade to Shine: New Poems

Pascha-themed Prayers

In Greek and Latin, and many other languages around the world, the word for the season and feast of Easter is a word clearly associated with "Passover," indelibly linking the Christian and Jewish holidays thematically. Pascha is both Greek and Latin for "Easter."

These prayers are most commonly found in the liturgies of Eastern Orthodox and Eastern Catholic churches. As you will see, in their recognition and celebration of Christ's triumph over death, they are often continuing the themes of Holy Saturday.

Imitate Him Whom You Worship

Pascha means the crossing-over,
and so the festival is called by this name.
For it was on this day that the children of Israel
crossed over out of Egypt,
and the Son of God crossed over
from this world to his Father.
What gain is it to celebrate
unless you imitate him whom you worship,
that is, unless you cross over from Egypt,
from the darkness of evildoing
to the light of virtue,
from the love of this world
to the love of your heavenly home?

—*St. Ambrose of Milan*

The Paschal Troparion

a hymn of one stanza

(repeat at least three times)

Christ is risen from the dead,
by death conquering death,
and to those in the tombs
granting life!

Troparia of the Resurrection

1

When You descended to death, O Life immortal, You destroyed Sheol with the splendor of Your divinity! And when from the depths You raised the dead, all the powers of heaven cried out: O Giver of Life, Christ our God, Glory to You!

2

Let the heavens rejoice! Let the earth be glad! For the Lord has shown strength with his arm! He has trampled down death by death! He has become the firstborn of the dead! He has delivered us from the depths of Sheol and has granted the world great mercy.

3

When the women disciples of the Lord learned from the angel the joyous message of Your Resurrection, they cast away the ancestral curse and elatedly told the apostles: Death is overthrown! Christ God is risen, granting the world great mercy!

4

Let us, the faithful, praise and worship the Word, Co-eternal with the Father and the Spirit, born for our salvation from the Virgin; for he willed to be lifted upon the cross in the flesh to endure death and to raise the dead by his glorious Resurrection!

5

The angelic powers were at your tomb; the guards became as dead men. Mary stood by Your grave, seeking Your most pure body. You captured Sheol, not being tempted by it. You came to the Virgin, granting Life. O Lord Who arose from the dead, glory to You!

6

By Your cross, You destroyed death! To the thief You granted Paradise! For the myrrh-bearers, You changed weeping into joy! And You commanded Your disciples, O Christ God, to proclaim that You are risen, granting the world great mercy.

7

From on high You descended, O merciful One! You accepted the three-day burial to free us from our sufferings! O Lord, our Life and Resurrection, glory to You!

Christ Is Risen!

"Christ is risen!" We cry out these words hundreds of times, in dozens of languages, in the weeks following Easter Sunday.

It was our own sins that enslaved us. "The wages of sin is death" (Rom. 6:23), and every child of Adam and Eve has since been born with a fatal susceptibility to sin, bound to pass through the door of death and into the shadowy realm of Hades. There could be no return to Paradise, for a cherub with a flaming sword stood to guard the gates (Gen. 3:24).

But God could not bear to see his beloved creatures, made in his own image and likeness (Gen. 1:26), damaged and dying. Christ came to rescue us, putting on our human nature and following our common course, even into the realm of Death. (It's the strategy we see in some action movies, where the hero rescues his imprisoned friend by first getting himself arrested.)

- "So will the Son of Man be three days and three nights in the heart of the earth" (Matt. 12:40).
- "He . . . descended into the lower parts of the earth" (Eph. 4:9).

- "[Christ was] . . . made alive in the spirit; in which he went and preached to the spirits in prison, who formerly did not obey" (1 Pet. 3:18–20).

- "The gospel was preached even to the dead, that though judged in the flesh like men, they might live in the spirit like God" (1 Pet. 4:6).

- "They shall gather them into a prison . . . and after many generations they shall be visited" (Isa. 24:22).

Christ went into Hades in the guise of a corpse—but, once there, he revealed his divinity. He flooded the darkness with his light and power, vanquishing the evil one and setting the captives free.

—*Frederica Mathewes-Green,*
from Welcome to the Orthodox Church:
An Introduction to Eastern Christianity

The More Earnest Prayer of Christ

And being in an agony he prayed more earnestly . . . —Luke 22:44

His last prayer in the garden began,
as most of his prayers began—*in earnest*, certainly;
but not without distraction, an habitual . . . what?
Distance? Well, yes, a sort of distance, or a mute
remove from the genuine distress he witnessed
in the endlessly grasping hands of multitudes
and, often enough, in his own embarrassing
circle of intimates. Even now, he could see
these where they slept, sprawled upon their robes or wrapped
among the arching olive trees. Still, something new,
unlikely, uncanny was commencing as he spoke.
As the divine in him contracted to an ache,
a throbbing in the throat, his vision blurred, his voice
grew thick and unfamiliar; his prayer—just before
it fell to silence—became uniquely earnest.
And in that moment—perhaps because it was so
new—he saw something, had his first taste of what
he would become, first pure taste of the body, and the blood.

—*Scott Cairns*

He Is Risen

After the Sabbath, as the first light of the new week dawned, Mary Magdalene and the other Mary came to keep vigil at the tomb. Suddenly the earth reeled and rocked under their feet as God's angel came down from heaven, came right up to where they were standing. He rolled back the stone and then sat on it. Shafts of lightning blazed from him. His garments shimmered snow-white. The guards at the tomb were scared to death. They were so frightened, they couldn't move.

The angel spoke to the women: "There is nothing to fear here. I know you're looking for Jesus, the One they nailed to the cross. He is not here. He was raised, just as he said. Come and look at the place where he was placed.

"Now, get on your way quickly and tell his disciples, 'He is risen from the dead. He is going on ahead of you to Galilee. You will see him there.' That's the message."

—*Matthew 28:1–7 (MSG)*

Easter Morning Greetings

"Christ is risen."

"He is risen indeed. Alleluia!"

(most Western Rite churches)

"Christ is risen!"

"Truly he is risen!"

(many Orthodox churches, often accompanied by a Paschal kiss)

Inspired by Luke 24:14–35

Christ the Lord Is Risen Today

Christ the Lord is risen today, Alleluia!
Earth and heaven in chorus say, Alleluia!
Raise your joys and triumphs high, Alleluia!
Sing, ye heavens, and earth reply, Alleluia!

Love's redeeming work is done, Alleluia!
Fought the fight, the battle won, Alleluia!
Death in vain forbids him rise, Alleluia!
Christ has opened paradise, Alleluia!

—*Rev. Charles Wesley*

Prayers for Ethiopian Orthodox Fasika *"Easter"*

Honor and Glory be to God forever and ever.

Honor and Glory be to the Holy Trinity forever and ever.

Honor and Glory be to the Life giver forever and ever.

Honor and Glory be to the commandments forever and ever.

Honor and Glory be to the kingdom forever and ever.

Honor and Glory be to Jesus forever and ever.

Honor and Glory be to Christ forever and ever.

Honor and Glory be to his suffering forever and ever.

Honor and Glory be to the cross forever and ever.

The Lord's Prayer: Our Father . . .

> —*Ethiopian Orthodox Christians celebrate Fasika*
> *after fasting fifty-five days. Many families still*
> *slaughter a sheep on Easter to begin their feast.*

This Day of Your Victory over Death

Today you, O Redeemer . . .
rise victoriously from the tomb to offer to us,
troubled by many threatening shadows,
your wish for joy and peace.
Those who are tempted by anxiety and desperation
turn to you, O Christ, our life and our guide,
to hear the proclamation of the hope that does not disappoint.
On this day of your victory over death,
may humanity find in you, O Lord, the courage to oppose
in solidarity the many evils that afflict it.

—Pope St. John Paul II
(April 11, 2004)

Giving Thanks for Easter Food

God of All Creation,

    as we rejoice in the Resurrection of our Lord, Jesus Christ,

    we place before You these gifts of Easter food.

We have prepared these traditional gifts and signs of life,

    bread, salt, and eggs, and we ask that You bless them.

Fill them, and through them, fill us, with Your Spirit,

May this bread nourish life.

May this salt preserve in us the hope of Easter morning.

May this egg be the eternal sign of the divine life hidden in us.

May all these blessed gifts of food be a source of grace to those

    who eat them.

Bless our Easter feast.

May our table be rich with the holiness, joy, and peace of You,

Father, Son, and Holy Spirit. Amen!

Your Resurrection Washed away Our Sins

It is only right,
with all the powers of our heart and mind,
to praise You, Father,
and Your only-begotten Son,
Our Lord Jesus Christ.
Father, by Your wondrous
condescension toward Your servants,
You gave up Your Son.
Jesus, You paid the debt of Adam for us
By Your Blood poured forth in lovingkindness.
You cleared away the darkness of sin
By Your magnificent and radiant Resurrection.
You broke the bonds of death
and rose from the grave as a conqueror.
You reconciled heaven and earth.
Our life had no hope of eternal happiness
before You redeemed us.
Your Resurrection has washed away our sins,
restored our innocence and brought us joy.
How inestimable is the tenderness
of Your love!

—*St. Gregory the Great*

Divine Love Revealed

This is a revelation of love that Jesus Christ, our endless joy, made in sixteen showings or revelations, in detail, of which:

The first is concerning His precious crowning with thorns; and therewith was included and described in detail the Trinity with the Incarnation and the unity between God and man's soul, with many beautiful showings of endless wisdom and teachings of love in which all the showings that follow are based and united.

The second showing is the discoloring of His fair face in symbolizing His dearworthy passion.

The third showing is that our Lord God—all Power, all Wisdom, all Love—just as truly as He has made everything that is, also truly He does and causes everything that is done.

The fourth showing is the scourging of His frail body with abundant shedding of His blood.

The fifth showing is that the Fiend is overcome by the precious Passion of Christ.

The sixth showing is the honor-filled favor of our Lord God with which He rewards all His blessed servants in heaven.

The seventh showing is a frequent experience of well and woe—the experience of "well" is grace-filled touching and enlightening, with true certainty of endless joy; the experience of "woe" is temptation by sadness and annoyance of our fleshly life—with spiritual understanding that even so we are protected safely in love—in woe as in well—by the goodness of God.

The eighth showing is the last pains of Christ and His cruel dying.

The ninth showing is about the delight which is in the blessed Trinity because of the cruel Passion of Christ and His regretful dying; in this joy and delight He wills we be comforted and made happy with Him until when we come to the fullness in heaven.

The tenth showing is that our Lord Jesus shows his blessed heart cloven in two in love.

The eleventh showing is a noble, spiritual showing of His dearworthy Mother.

The twelfth showing is that our Lord is all supreme Being.

The thirteenth showing is that our Lord God wills that we have great regard for all the deeds that He has done in the great splendor of creating all things, and of the excellency of creating man (who is above all His other works), and of the precious amends that He has made for man's sin, turning all our blame into endless honor, and here also our Lord says: "Behold and see; for by the same Power, Wisdom, and Goodness that I have done all this, by that same Power, Wisdom, and Goodness I shall make well all that is not well, and thou thyself shalt see it." And in this showing He wills that we keep us in the Faith and truth of Holy Church, not wishing to be aware of His secrets now, except as is proper for us in this life.

The fourteenth showing is that our Lord is the foundation of our prayer. Herein were seen two elements that He wills both be equally great: the one is righteous prayer, the other is sure trust; and in these ways our prayer delights Him, and He of His goodness fulfills it.

The fifteenth showing is that we shall without delay be taken from all our pain and from all our woe and, of His goodness, we shall come up above where we shall have our Lord Jesus for our recompense and be filled with joy and bliss in heaven.

The sixteenth showing is that the blessed Trinity our Creator, in Christ Jesus our Savior, endlessly dwells in our soul, honorably governing and controlling all things, powerfully and wisely saving and protecting us for the sake of love; and that we shall not be overcome by our Enemy.

…For the Trinity is God, God is the Trinity; the Trinity is our Maker, the Trinity is our Keeper, the Trinity is our everlasting Lover, the Trinity is our endless Joy and Bliss, through our Lord Jesus Christ and in our Lord Jesus Christ.

…Our good Lord showed to me a spiritual vision of His simple loving. I saw which He is to us everything that is good and comfortable for us. He is our clothing that for love enwraps us, holds us, and all encloses us because of His tender love, so that He may never leave us.

—*Julian of Norwich*

Raise Us Up

God our Father,
by raising Christ your Son
you conquered the power of death
and opened for us the way to eternal life.
Let our celebration today
raise us up and renew our lives
by the Spirit that is within us.
Grant this through our Lord Jesus Christ, your Son,
who lives and reigns with you and Holy Spirit,
one God, for ever and ever.

—*Traditional Catholic prayer for this day*

Thanks to God

Blessed be the God and Father of our Lord Jesus Christ! By his great mercy he has given us a new birth into a living hope through the resurrection of Jesus Christ from the dead, and into an inheritance that is imperishable, undefiled, and unfading, kept in heaven for you, who are being protected by the power of God through faith for a salvation ready to be revealed in the last time. In this you rejoice, even if now for a little while you have had to suffer various trials, so that the genuineness of your faith—being more precious than gold that, though perishable, is tested by fire— may be found to result in praise and glory and honor when Jesus Christ is revealed. Although you have not seen him, you love him; and even though you do not see him now, you believe in him and rejoice with an indescribable and glorious joy, for you are receiving the outcome of your faith, the salvation of your souls.

—1 Peter 1:3–9

Walk in Newness of Life

Dear God,

Thank you that I have been buried with Christ by baptism into death, so that, just as Christ was raised from the dead by the glory of the Father, so I too might walk in newness of life. For if I have been united with him in a death like his, I will certainly be united with him in a resurrection like his.

—See Romans 6:4–5

Traditional Polish Prayer of Gratitude

Living Bread, who came down from heaven, and in the Holy Communion that gives life to the world, bless this bread in memory of the bread with which You fed the devout people who listened to You in the desert, and in memory of the blessed dishes You consumed with the Apostles during the Last Supper.

Lamb of God, who has conquered evil and cleansed the world of sin, bless these meats, sausages, and other food in which we shall partake in memory of the Paschal Lamb. Bless also this salt that it may preserve us from spoiling and corruption.

Dear Christ, our life and Resurrection, bless these eggs, the sign of new life, so that when we share them with our loved ones, we might also mutually share in the joy of your presence among us.

May we all attain Your eternal feast there, where you live and reign forever and ever. Amen.

> *—At the end of this prayer, the priest blesses the food by sprinkling holy water over the baskets, while the faithful make the Sign of the Cross.*

Prayers for Eastertide

Alleluia Is Our Song!

We do not pretend that life is all beauty. We are aware of darkness and sin, of poverty and pain. But we know Jesus has conquered sin and passed through his own pain to the glory of the Resurrection. And we live in the light of his Paschal Mystery – the mystery of his Death and Resurrection. We are an Easter people and Alleluia is our song! We are not looking for a shallow joy but rather a joy that comes from faith, that grows through unselfish love.

—Pope St. John Paul II
(November 30, 1986)

The Gift of Your Easter Joy

We praise you, Christ Jesus.

The light of your face, the light of the resurrection shines in our heart and in the very darkness of humanity.

We entrust to you those who are suffering from the consequences of natural disasters, and also, those who are seeking justice and are victims of violence across the world.

In the face of suffering and death we are speechless.

But in looking towards you, Christ, the trust of faith can be born and reborn in us.

The gift of your Easter joy gives us the courage to hope once again, rooted in God's own faithfulness towards us.

—An Easter prayer from the Taizé Community,
translated from Arabic

Miriam's Prayer of Praise

When the horses of Pharaoh with his chariots and his chariot drivers went into the sea, the LORD brought back the waters of the sea upon them; but the Israelites walked through the sea on dry ground. Then the prophet Miriam, Aaron's sister, took a tambourine in her hand; and all the women went out after her with tambourines and with dancing. And Miriam sang to them:

> "Sing to the LORD, for he has triumphed gloriously;
> horse and rider he has thrown into the sea."

—Exodus 15:19–21

Jesus's Prayer for Unity

I ask not only on behalf of these, but also on behalf of those who will believe in me through their word, that they may all be one. As you, Father, are in me and I am in you, may they also be in us, so that the world may believe that you have sent me. The glory that you have given me I have given them, so that they may be one, as we are one, I in them and you in me, that they may become completely one, so that the world may know that you have sent me and have loved them even as you have loved me.

—John 17:20–23

Prayers for the Octave of Easter

The Lord has risen from the dead, as he said.
Let us all exult and rejoice,
for he reigns for all eternity.
Alleluia.

This is the day the Lord has made.
Let us rejoice and be glad.
Alleluia.

*—The Octave of Easter refers to the eight-day
festival period in Western churches beginning on
Easter Sunday, concluding the following Sunday.*

You Give Us a New Life in the Spirit

God of mercy,
you wash away our sins in water,
you give us a new birth in the Spirit,
and redeem us in the blood of Christ.
As we celebrate Christ's resurrection,
increase our awareness of these blessings,
and renew your gift of life within us.
We ask this through our Lord Jesus Christ, your Son,
who lives and reigns with you and the Holy Spirit,
one God, for ever and ever.
Amen.

Join the Saints in Heaven

Almighty and ever-living God,
give us new strength
from the courage of Christ our shepherd,
and lead us to join the saints in heaven,
where he lives and reigns with you and the Holy Spirit,
one God, for ever and ever.
Amen.

We Look with Hope

God our Father,
may we look forward with hope
to our resurrection,
for you have made us your sons and daughters,
and restored the joy of our youth.
We ask this through our Lord Jesus Christ, your Son,
who lives and reigns with you and the Holy Spirit,
one God, for ever and ever.
Amen.

—Catholic collects for the Sundays in Easter

Essential Easter Prayers

Lord, You Are So Patient

Lord, you are so patient with us. You brought us through Easter when we rejoiced at the news of the resurrection of your Son our Savior. You were with us in the upper room when we remained hidden out of our fears, sharing with Thomas our doubts and anxieties. Now you come to us on the road. You come to us in our everyday lives, moving out of our traditional settings of worship into the work world. But we aren't always ready for you and don't always see you or feel your presence. We let so many things crowd in on our lives and these intrusions blot out our awareness of your presence. Forgive our inattentiveness and our stubbornness. Help us keep our hearts open to you, to see and tell the good things you have done in our lives. For we ask this in Jesus's name. Amen.

—*A prayer of the African Methodist Episcopal Church*

Easter Psalms

O LORD, our Sovereign, how majestic is your name
in all the earth!
You have set your glory above the heavens.
Out of the mouths of babes and infants you have
founded a bulwark because of your foes,
to silence the enemy and the avenger.
When I look at your heavens, the work of your fingers,
the moon and the stars that you have established;
what are human beings that you are mindful of them,
mortals that you care for them?
Yet you have made them a little lower than God,
and crowned them with glory and honor.
You have given them dominion over the works of your hands;
you have put all things under their feet, all sheep
and oxen, and also the beasts of the field, the birds of
the air, and the fish of the sea, whatever passes along
the paths of the seas.
O LORD, our Sovereign, how majestic is
your name in all the earth!

—Psalm 8

The LORD is king, he is robed in majesty;
the LORD is robed, he is girded with strength.
He has established the world; it shall never be moved;
your throne is established from of old;
you are from everlasting.
The floods have lifted up, O LORD,
the floods have lifted up their voice;
the floods lift up their roaring.
More majestic than the thunders of mighty waters,
more majestic than the waves of the sea,
majestic on high is the LORD!
Your decrees are very sure;
holiness befits your house,
O LORD, forevermore.

—*Psalm 93*

Praise the LORD!
Praise, O servants of the LORD;
praise the name of the LORD.
Blessed be the name of the LORD
from this time on and forevermore.
From the rising of the sun to its setting
the name of the LORD is to be praised.
The LORD is high above all nations,
and his glory above the heavens.
Who is like the LORD our God, who is seated on high,
who looks far down on the heavens and the earth?
He raises the poor from the dust,
and lifts the needy from the ash heap,
to make them sit with princes,
with the princes of his people.
He gives the barren woman a home,
making her the joyous mother of children.
Praise the LORD!

—*Psalm 113*

Essential EasterPrayers

A Hymn to be Sung

And can it be, that I should gain
    An interest in the Savior's blood!
Died he for me?—Who caused his pain!
    For me?—Who him to death pursued.
Amazing love! How can it be
That thou, my God, shouldst die for me?

'Tis mystery all! The immortal dies!
    Who can explore his strange design?
In vain the first-born seraph tries
    To sound the depths of love divine.
'Tis mercy all! Let earth adore;
Let angel minds enquire no more.

He left his Father's throne above,
   (So free, so infinite his grace!)
Emptied himself of all but love,
   And bled for Adam's helpless race:
'Tis mercy all, immense and free!
For O my God! It found out me!

Long my imprisoned spirit lay,
   Fast bound in sin and nature's night:
Thine eye diffused a quickening ray;
   I woke; the dungeon flamed with light;
My chains fell off, my heart was free,
I rose, went forth, and followed thee.

Still the small inward voice I hear,
    That whispers all my sins forgiven;
the atoning blood is near,
    That quenched the wrath of hostile heaven:
I feel the life his wounds impart;
I feel my Savior in my heart.

No condemnation now I dread,
    Jesus, and all in him, is mine:
Alive in him, my living head,
    And clothed in righteousness divine,
Bold I approach the eternal throne,
And claim the crown, through Christ, my own.

—*Rev. Charles Wesley*

Prayer to the Sacred Heart of Jesus

O most Sacred, most loving Heart of Jesus,
Thou art concealed in the Holy Eucharist,
    and Thou beatest for us still.
I worship Thee with all my best love and awe,
    with my fervent affection, with my most subdued,
    most resolved will.
O my God, when Thou dost condescend to suffer me
    to receive Thee, to eat and drink Thee, and Thou
    for a while takest up Thy abode within me,
O make my heart beat with Thy Heart.
Purify it of all that is earthly, all that is proud and sensual,
    all that is hard and cruel, of all perversity,
    of all disorder, of all deadness.
So fill it with Thee, that neither the events of the day nor
    the circumstances of the time may have power to ruffle it,
    but that in Thy love and Thy fear it may have peace.
Amen.

—*St. John Henry Newman*

Regina Caeli, "Queen of Heaven"

Queen of heaven, rejoice, alleluia.

The Son you merited to bear, alleluia,

Has risen as he said, alleluia.

Pray to God for us, alleluia.

May the Cross Ever Remind Us of Thy Great Love

Eternal and everlasting God, who art the Father of all mankind,
  as we turn aside from the hurly-burly of everyday living,
  may our hearts and souls, yea our very spirits, be lifted
  upward to Thee, for it is from Thee that all blessing cometh.
Keep us ever mindful of our dependence upon Thee, for without
  Thee our efforts are but naught.
We pray for Thy divine guidance as we travel the highways of life.
We pray for more courage.
We pray for more faith and above all we pray for more love.
May we somehow come to understand the true meaning of Thy
  love as revealed to us in the life, death and resurrection of
  Thy son and our Lord and Master, Jesus Christ.
May the cross ever remind us of Thy great love, for greater love
  no man hath given.
This is our supreme example, O God.
May we be constrained to follow in the name and spirit of Jesus,
  we pray.

—Coretta Scott King

CONTRIBUTOR BIOGRAPHIES

The African Methodist Episcopal Church, or AME, is headquartered in Nashville, Tennessee. The prayer "Lord, You Are So Patient" was offered as a free resource from their Christian Education Department for the Third Sunday of Easter, April 26, 2020.

St. Ambrose of Milan was the bishop of Milan, a theologian, mentor to St. Augustine, and one of the most important Christians of the late Roman Empire.

St. Augustine of Hippo was a bishop and theologian of the late fourth and early fifth centuries. Two of his books, *Confessions* and *The City of God*, are among the most-read spiritual books in history.

St. Basil the Great is also known as Basil of Caesarea, for the city in Asia Minor (today's Kayseri, Turkey) where he was bishop. He fought heresy and was one of the Cappadocian Fathers.

Dietrich Bonhoeffer was a Lutheran pastor who ministered in Harlem in the US, and throughout Europe, but returned to Nazi Germany to join in the resistance to Hitler, who ordered his execution in 1945. He is the author of several books including *The Cost of Discipleship*.

Scott Cairns is an award-winning contemporary American poet. This poem is taken from the Paraclete Press book *Slow Pilgrim: The Collected Poems*.

Bl. (Blessed) Charles de Foucauld served in the French Army and as an explorer before becoming a Catholic priest and a hermit in the desert of north Africa. He was martyred in 1916.

St. Gregory the Great was also Pope Gregory I. He is known as the "Father of Christian Worship" because of all the divine liturgy he authored. He is one of the Latin Fathers and a Doctor of the Church.

Coretta Scott King (1927–2006) was an activist, civil rights leader, author, and wife of Dr. Martin Luther King, Jr.

St. John Henry Newman was an English priest, theologian, and university president. He was probably the most influential Christian of the nineteenth century, and his writings had a great influence on the participants of the Second Vatican Council.

St. Pope John Paul II was the leader of the worldwide Roman Catholic Church for twenty-seven years (1978–2005). His writings include spirituality, theology, encyclicals, and poems. He is also one of the most traveled world leaders in history.

Julian of Norwich (ca. 1342–1416) lived in Norwich, England as an anchoress, attached to a church, counseling people through a small window. She received sixteen revelations or "showings" of Christ's Passion; the prayer here is derived from the eighth.

Frederica Mathewes-Green has been a regular commentator for National Public Radio and a podcaster for Ancient Faith Radio. She's the author of many books including *Facing East* and *Welcome to the Orthodox Church*.

Jill Peláez-Baumgaertner is Professor of English Emerita at Wheaton College. She has been a Fulbright scholar and a poet for many decades. *From Shade to Shine: New Poems* publishes late in 2021.

Cardinal Luis Antonio Tagle is the former Archbishop of Manila and current Prefect of the Congregation of Evangelization of Peoples, appointed by Pope Francis.

The Taizé Community is an ecumenical gathering of Christian pilgrims that originated in Taizé (part of Burgundy) France in 1940. More than 100,000 people visit the original community each year, and there are related communities in many countries throughout the world.

St. Teresa of Avila was a sixteenth-century Spanish Carmelite nun, abbess, mystic, writer, and religious reformer. Her works, including *The Interior Castle* and *The Way of Perfection*, are still popular today.

St. Teresa of Calcutta, or "Mother Teresa," won the Nobel Peace Prize and lived most of her long life among the poorest of the poor in India. This quotation is from the Paraclete Press book *I Loved Jesus in the Night: Teresa of Calcutta—A Secret Revealed*, by Paul Murray.

Harriet Tubman was a former slave who became a prominent abolitionist and political activist for the rights of Black people in the United States. Known for her extraordinary faith and courage, she conducted many dangerous missions to save enslaved people before the Civil War and served as a scout for the Union Army during the conflict. She was nicknamed "Moses."

Suzanne Underwood Rhodes, of Fayetteville, Arkansas, is a poet of several collections including *Flying Yellow: New and Selected Poem*s, publishing in 2021 with Paraclete Poetry.

Christine Valters Paintner is the online Abbess of Abbey of the Arts, and a bestselling author of spirituality and poetry including *The Soul of a Pilgrim* and *The Wisdom of Wild Grace: Poems*. She lives in Ireland.

Rev. Charles Wesley (1707–1788) was a leader of the Methodist movement in England, and a prolific hymn writer.

ABOUT PARACLETE PRESS

WHO WE ARE

As the publishing arm of the Community of Jesus, Paraclete Press presents a full expression of Christian belief and practice—from Catholic to Evangelical, from Protestant to Orthodox, reflecting the ecumenical charism of the Community and its dedication to sacred music, the fine arts, and the written word. We publish books, recordings, sheet music, and video/DVDs that nourish the vibrant life of the church and its people.

WHAT WE ARE DOING

BOOKS | PARACLETE PRESS BOOKS show the richness and depth of what it means to be Christian. While Benedictine spirituality is at the heart of who we are and all that we do, our books reflect the Christian experience across many cultures, time periods, and houses of worship.

We have many series, including *Paraclete Essentials; Paraclete Fiction; Paraclete Poetry; Paraclete Giants;* and for children and adults, *All God's Creatures,* books about animals and faith; and *San Damiano Books,* focusing on Franciscan spirituality. Others include *Voices from the Monastery* (men and women monastics writing about living a spiritual life today), *Active Prayer,* and new for young readers: *The Pope's Cat.* We also specialize in gift books for children on the occasions of Baptism and First Communion, as well as other important times in a child's life, and books that bring creativity and liveliness to any adult spiritual life.

The MOUNT TABOR BOOKS series focuses on the arts and literature as well as liturgical worship and spirituality; it was created in conjunction with the Mount Tabor Ecumenical Centre for Art and Spirituality in Barga, Italy.

MUSIC | PARACLETE PRESS DISTRIBUTES RECORDINGS of the internationally acclaimed choir *Gloriæ Dei Cantores,* the *Gloriæ Dei Cantores Schola,* and the other instrumental artists of the *Arts Empowering Life Foundation.*

PARACLETE PRESS IS THE EXCLUSIVE NORTH AMERICAN DISTRIBUTOR for the Gregorian chant recordings from St. Peter's Abbey in Solesmes, France. Paraclete also carries all of the Solesmes chant publications for Mass and the Divine Office, as well as their academic research publications.

In addition, PARACLETE PRESS SHEET MUSIC publishes the work of today's finest composers of sacred choral music, annually reviewing over 1,000 works and releasing between 40 and 60 works for both choir and organ.

VIDEO | Our video/DVDs offer spiritual help, healing, and biblical guidance for a broad range of life issues including grief and loss, marriage, forgiveness, facing death, understanding suicide, bullying, addictions, Alzheimer's, and Christian formation.

Learn more about us at our website:
www.paracletepress.com
or phone us toll-free at 1.800.451.5006

SCAN
TO
READ